Inside a Rock Band

By Deb Barnes

The Child's World®
www.childsworld.com

Published in the United States of America by The Child's World®
P.O. Box 326 • Chanhassen, MN 55317-0326
800-599-READ • www.childsworld.com

Thanks to Jetpack UK for letting me "be with the band."—D. B.

ACKNOWLEDGMENTS

The Child's World®: Mary Berendes, Publishing Director

Produced by Shoreline Publishing Group LLC
President / Editorial Director: James Buckley, Jr.
Designer: Tom Carling, carlingdesign.com
Cover Art: Slimfilms
Copy Editor: Beth Adelman

Photo Credits
All photos by Ed Rode, except the following:
Courtesy Jetpack UK: 11, 15, 23; Getty Images: 29;
Photos.com: 3, 7, 9, 22.

LIBRARY OF CONGRESS CATALOGING-IN-PUBLICATION DATA

Barnes, Deb.
  Inside a rock band / by Deb Barnes.
      p. cm. — (Girls rock!)
  Includes bibliographical references (p.   ) and index.
  ISBN 1-59296-745-0 (library bound : alk. paper)
  1. Rock music—History and criticism—Juvenile literature.
  2. Rock groups—Juvenile literature. I. Title. II. Series.
ML3534.B323 2006
781.66—dc22

                                        2006001642

27.10

CONTENTS

DO YOU LOVE Music?

Do you love music? Do you like listening to the radio or your MP3 player? Do you like to sing along with your favorite songs and pretend you're a famous rock star? Join the club!

Being a musician looks like a blast, but it can be a lot of work, too. Meet Jetpack UK, a group of guys who are trying to make it in the music business.

They dream of hearing their songs on the radio. These guys know what it's really like to be in a rock band . . . and they've given us this special peek into their world. So get ready to rock!

Here are Stephen, Sean, Brian, and David, the four guys from Jetpack UK.

Sean Williams is the lead singer for the band.

A bass guitar plays lower notes and helps keep the beat.

There are four members of Jetpack UK. Sean Williams sings and plays guitar. Stephen Jerkins plays guitar and keyboards. David Dewese plays **bass** (BASE) **guitar.** And Brian Fuzzell plays the drums.

When they were just kids learning to play music, Sean, Stephen, David, and Brian dreamed of being rock stars.

If you want to be in a band, you need to learn how to play an **instrument**. "My dad made me take guitar lessons," says David. "Now I'm glad he did!" As they got older and learned to play better, the four musicians started putting bands together.

Playing an instrument is a great thing to learn—and if you ever want to be in a band, you'll be ready to go!

Can't Rock Without It

Nothing says "rock" like an electric guitar. It can be strummed or picked for sounds that stand out from the rest of the song. Electric guitars have a solid body and six strings. They're quiet by themselves, but they plug into **amplifiers** that make them much louder.

"Record labels" are music companies. The name comes from the glued-on labels that listed songs and musicians on old vinyl records.

To become **professional** musicians, all four guys moved to Nashville, Tennessee. Nashville is home to lots of recording studios, **record labels,** and other music businesses.

Music Cities

Music is big business! There are many different parts to it, too—from finding talented musicians, to recording the music, to getting people to play it on the radio and buy the CDs. People can make music anywhere, but Los Angeles, New York City, and Nashville are home to some of the world's biggest music companies. There are music businesses in other cities, too, from Atlanta to Chicago.

Nashville is where Sean and Stephen met David and Brian. In 2003, they formed Jetpack UK.

Musicians have to give up some things to succeed. They have to practice when they'd rather be out with their friends, for instance.

Lots of people have left their homes and moved to Nashville to follow their dream of a music career.

GETTING TO Work

Because Jetpack UK isn't a famous band yet, the guys don't make a lot of money from their performances. They all have **day jobs** to earn enough to live on. That means that after they work during the day, they do "band work" at night.

Sean writes most of the group's songs. "I write songs every day," he says.

"They're not always good songs, but it's important to practice my writing every day. I usually start with the **melody**, and work out the **lyrics** as I go."

As you can see from his notebook pages, Sean often has to try many words before he finds just the right lyrics.

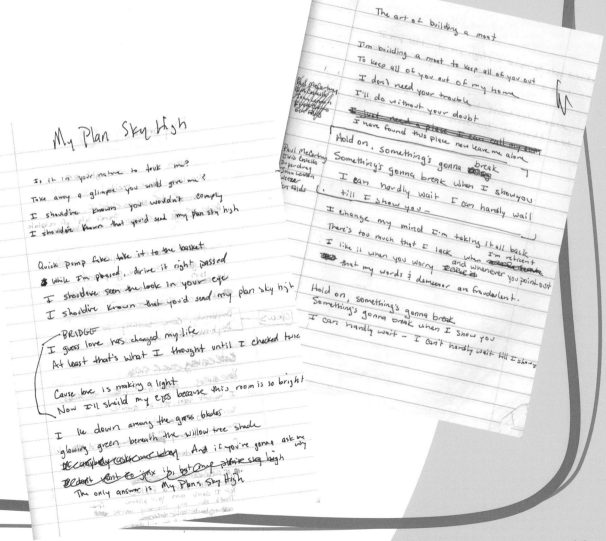

All the band members practice their instruments every day to keep up their skills.

They also get together twice a week in David's basement to **rehearse** together. They practice playing the songs they already know, and they learn new ones. Sometimes Sean brings in a song he's just written, and the guys learn to play it.

Together they can also add their own special touches to each song. They also learn to sing the **harmony** parts with Sean.

Practice helps for singing different notes together, in harmony.

Being in a band isn't just about playing music. The guys spend part of their time calling clubs to try to **book** shows. Lots of bands are trying to get **gigs** in the same clubs.

Stephen works on his keyboard skills to get ready for an upcoming gig.

Jetpack UK members send out information about their group and CDs of their music. They often have to convince club owners to hire them to play a show.

The guys already have several CDs they've made on their own. They paid for time to record in a studio with a **producer**. They sell their CDs at shows and on their Web site. They also give CDs to the managers of clubs where they'd like to play.

Here are a couple of Jetpack UK CD covers.

Planning a list of songs to play at each show takes a lot of trial and error. This whiteboard shows one such "set list."

Jetpack UK wants to play for the public as much as possible so the band will get more fans. Having fans makes it easier to get gigs! And doing more shows gives the band a better chance of being seen by someone from a record label.

Most bands want to sign a **contract** with a record label, because then the label pays for the group to record a new CD.

Do you have to sign a contract to have a music career? No, but without one, it's tough to make a living in a rock band. You'll have to keep your day job.

The company also helps send the CD to radio stations and music stores so that more people will buy it. After they're signed to a label, members of a band can often give up their day jobs for a while and make music full time. Awesome!

Jetpack UK hasn't signed to a record label yet, but they have taken another step forward in the music business—they just hired a **manager,** Brian Darnell.

A manager takes care of the business side of a band. That includes booking the band into bigger clubs, running ads for shows, and working hard to get the band signed up with a record label. Brian likes Jetpack UK's music and thinks he can help the group become better known.

"We hope Brian will get our music to people who might give us a record deal and to movie people who might use our music in a film or TV show," says Sean. In general, Brian will try to get Jetpack UK's music to everyone!

You are there! The band has just signed Brian (center) to be their manager!

TIME TO
Play!

Being a musician takes commitment and lots of work! Because they spend so much time rehearsing and playing gigs, band members don't have much time to be with friends.

Plus, being a musician costs money — you always have to buy new guitar strings or get your equipment fixed. But none of that matters when you think about the fun part of being a rocker— playing for the crowd!

After all their hard work, the fun part finally begins— Jetpack UK takes the stage in Nashville.

Playing music for more people means traveling— a lot. Most bands play gigs in lots of different cities and states.

Famous bands often travel by plane or in their own bus, but bands that are just starting out, like Jetpack UK, usually drive

Gear Up

Putting on a rock show means taking along a lot of gear. Along with instruments, bands have to bring their own amplifiers (left).

their own cars. If the town is far away from home, the guys stay in a hotel. After the show, they look around the town and eat at local restaurants. To pass the time, they try to find unusual museums or odd places to visit. Road-tripping, or traveling with the band, can be fun!

Ah, the glamorous life of a rock star! When they're big stars, they won't have to carry their own instruments.

Rock-star view: Here's what drummer Brian Fuzzell sees during a show.

Once the guys get to the town where they're playing, they check into a hotel or visit the club where they're going to play. At the club, they set up all their gear.

When they're all plugged in, they **tune** their instruments. Then they practice for a bit to make sure the club's sound system works well.

Until they become famous enough to **headline** their own shows, Jetpack UK will usually share the **bill** with other bands. That means several bands will play at a club in one night. Jetpack UK might play for an hour or so, followed by another band. "We usually do 12 to 15 songs in a show," says Sean.

Instruments such as guitars have to be adjusted, or tuned, each time you play them to make sure they sound right.

Finally, after all the preparation and practice and time and work, the lights go up in the club and it's time to play.

Sometimes the band turns on some funny music as they walk onto the stage, to make the audience laugh. Usually they just launch into one of their loud, fast songs to start the evening with a bang.

Between songs, they chat with the crowd or tease each other about their clothes.

And just so the audience doesn't forget, Sean always reminds them, "We're Jetpack UK. We hope you enjoy the show!"

Hit it! Sean and David play the first notes of the night.

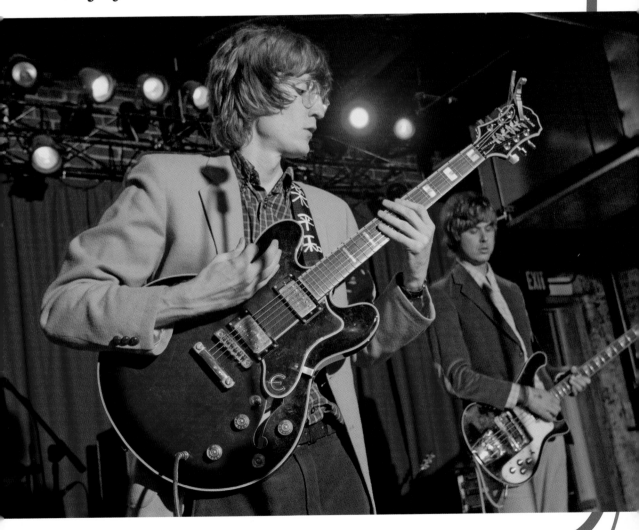

The show rocks on for about an hour. The crowd loves the music! Sean and the guys have a great time. All that practice in the basement has made them play perfectly.

After a quick **encore** (ON-kore), the show's over. Time to get back on the road.

Being a musician is hard, but most musicians will tell you it's all worth it. The joy of performing and the thrill of seeing people enjoy your music are things you can't get from most jobs.

After the show is over, if the crowd cheers loudly enough, the band will play another song—the encore.

"The best part for me is when people tell me one of my songs touched them or really meant something to them," says Sean. "That's why I do this. It's like I have to do it . . . it's part of me. I won't be happy unless I'm making music." Rock on!

This is Jetpack UK's goal—to play their music in front of a huge crowd like this one.

GLOSSARY

amplifiers   electronic devices that make sounds louder

bass guitar   a four-stringed guitar that usually plays lower notes

bill   the lineup of performers at a concert or club

book   in this case, to make a deal to play at a club or concert

contract   a legal agreement between people or companies that spells out what both sides will do

day job   regular work to support a hobby or other interests

encore   an extra song played at the end of a show if the audience wants to hear more

gig   a show-business term for a show or a job

harmony   different notes played or sung at the same time

headline   to be the most important or famous act in a show

instrument   anything used to play music

lyrics   the words to a song

manager   someone who takes care of the business side of a band

melody   the tune of a song

producer   the person in charge of recording a CD

professional   a person who is paid to do a job

record label   a company that pays for musicians to record their music, and in return gets some of the money made from selling the music

rehearse   practice, usually for a performance

tune   adjust an instrument so that it produces the right tones

FIND OUT MORE

BOOKS

Create Your Own Girl Band
by Janet Hoggarth
(Scholastic/Chicken House, New York), 2001
A hip guide packed with tips on everything from writing lyrics to creating dance steps and performing.

Kids Make Music: Clapping & Tapping from Bach to Rock!
by Avery Hart, Paul Mantell, and Loretta Trezzo Braren
(Williamson Publishing, Charlotte, VT), 1993
A hands-on approach to making music that includes sections on both classical and rock music.

So, You Wanna Be a Rock Star: How to Create Music, Get Gigs, and Maybe Even Make It Big!
by Stephen Anderson and Eric Stefani
(Beyond Words Publishing, Hillsboro, OR), 2002
A real-life rocker takes you behind the scenes with his band and his tour.

WEB SITES

Visit our home page for lots of links about music and musicians:
www.childsworld.com/links

Note to Parents, Teachers, and Librarians: We routinely check our Web links to make sure they're safe, active sites—so encourage your readers to check them out!

INDEX

DEB BARNES is a kids' magazine editor in Nashville, Tennessee. Although the rock band she joined during college never made the big time, she still loves music, as well as sports, traveling, and home decorating.